W9-CNZ-061

GALAXIES

BY THE SAME AUTHOR

Colonies in Orbit
Eavesdropping on Space
Harnessing the Sun
Thirty-Two Moons
The Tiny Planets

The lovely spiral galaxy NGC 4565 in the constellation Coma Berenices (Bernice's Hair), seen edge on. The dark, obscuring dust lane that runs through the disk is similar to that near the central plane of our own Milky Way galaxy. *Lick Observatory*

DAVID C. KNIGHT

GALAXIES
ISLANDS IN SPACE

illustrated with 36 photographs and diagrams

WILLIAM MORROW AND COMPANY
New York 1979

Library of Congress Cataloging in Publication Data

Knight, David C
Galaxies, islands in space.

1. Galaxies—Juvenile literature. I. Title.
QB857.K54 523.1'12 78-21625
ISBN 0-688-22180-7
ISBN 0-688-32180-1

Printed in the United States of America.
First Edition
1 2 3 4 5 6 7 8 9 10

This book is for Constance Weed Schronk.

CONTENTS

GALAXIES

1 THE MILKY WAY

Hurtling through space at fantastic speeds are the largest collections of matter known to science, the galaxies. Galaxies are vast islands of stars. They are scattered throughout the universe. No one knows how many of these islands of stars lie beyond the one we inhabit, but there are surely many billions of them. Some lie so far away that no earthly telescope could produce an image of them. Beyond them may lie still more starry islands, extending to the very edges of the universe itself.

The Earth and the system of sun and planets to which it belongs are a part of one of these galaxies. It is an infinitely tiny part, no more than a speck of dust in a gigantic rotating wheel composed of billions of stars. This great wheel not only rotates, it also has a forward directional motion. At this moment, all of us—and all the rest of the stars in our galaxy—are rushing through space at more than 300 miles a second. Moreover, astronomers believe that other galaxies are traveling even faster. Some are thought to be approaching the speed of light itself, which is 186,000 miles a second.

If you look up at the sky on a clear night, you can see a faint glowing band of stars extending from one horizon to the other. It slashes across the sky line like a shimmering river of flowing milk. That is how it looked to the ancient Greeks, who gave our island of stars its name, the Milky Way. *Galaxy* in Greek means *milk.* The light produced by this trail of milk is the accumulated light of billions of stars. Formerly it was thought that the Milky Way, or as it is also called, The Galaxy, contained about 100 billion stars. Now scientists think there are closer to 250 billion. Some are new stars recently born from vast quantities of gas and dust com-

A famous spiral galaxy, M 81 in the constellation Ursa Major (The Great Bear). *Kitt Peak Observatory*

ing together and glowing in space. Others are dying stars, their nuclear fires spent in old age. Still others, like our own sun, are vigorous middle-aged stars.

It is important to realize that all the stars we can see with the naked eye as well as all those that can be seen through ordinary telescopes are part of The Galaxy. It is immense

A region of the Milky Way showing a small star cloud.
Lick Observatory

indeed. Yet it is possible to see several galaxies beyond our own without a telescope. Look carefully at the constellation Andromeda, which you can find with the aid of any star chart. Just above the middle star in this constellation is a faint hazy patch. This patch is the great galaxy in Andromeda. It is, in fact, the farthest object that can be seen with the naked eye—over eight million trillion miles from Earth. It is also the nearest large galaxy to our own.

Most other visible hazy patches of matter are inside the Milky Way. They are great clouds of gas called "nebulae." You can see a nebula through a good pair of binoculars. Train the binoculars on the constellation Orion, the Hunter. Now find the bottom star in the mythical hunter's sword. You'll see the nebula as a hazy patch just above this star.

If you could fly outside our galaxy in a spaceship, how would the Milky Way look? If you were either above or below it, you would see a great spiral disk of dust, gas, and stars rotating about a bright hub. If you flew to the thin edge of The Galaxy, you would see it has the shape of an immense lens with a big bulge at its center. You would also see that the edges of our galaxy taper off into the space around it.

Back on Earth we see our galaxy in a different way. Since we are part of it, we are looking at it from the inside outward. When we look at the river of milk in the night sky, we are looking toward the densest group of stars that form the lens shape of our galaxy. In other words, we are looking edge

on at the stars, dust, and gas that form the thickness of the Milky Way. However, since the Milky Way is never all above the horizon at one time, we see it as an arch across the sky.

In the photograph of The Galaxy on page 16, you can see that the Milky Way is split by a long, dark lane and that in several places there are dark spots. These spots are huge clouds of gas and dust that hide the stars that are farther away. There are also bright clouds, which are great clusters of many thousands of stars.

How big is The Galaxy? Astronomers do not use mere miles to measure objects and distances in the vastness of space. The numbers of zeroes needed to express such distances in miles are so great that they become meaningless. So astronomers use light-years. A light-year is the distance that light travels in one year, about six trillion miles. As seen from edge on, the bulge at the center of The Galaxy is about 20,000 light-years thick. Measured from one tapered end to the other—its diameter—the Milky Way is about 100,000 light-years in length.

Our galaxy is also rotating around its center. Naturally our

The Great Andromeda Galaxy, M 31 (NGC 224). One of the most magnificent of all galaxies, M 31's bright nucleus can be seen with the naked eye. The galaxy's two companions are dwarf elliptical galaxies, NGC 205 and 221. All three are members of our local group of galaxies. *Hale Observatories*

sun as a part of The Galaxy is rotating along with it, as are the Earth and other planets. Right at this minute we are moving around the distant center of the Milky Way at about 150 miles per second. However, so gigantic is The Galaxy as a whole that our solar system takes over 200 million years to complete one full trip around the galactic center.

The sun itself is nowhere near the center. It is about two-thirds of the way from it, or about 30,000 light-years away. It lies in one of the great curving arms that trail around the center of our galaxy. Depending on their position in The Galaxy, some stars take longer than others to make the full trip around the galactic center.

The center of our Milky Way is still a mystery to astronomers. It is the gravitational nucleus, or middle part, about which our sun and the other billions of stars composing The Galaxy rotate. Beyond that fact, not much is known. Indeed, we know less about the center of our own galaxy than about the centers, or nuclei, of many distant galaxies. Vast clouds of dust lie between our galactic center and us, making observation of it difficult. Nevertheless, astronomers are gen-

The Great Nebula in the constellation Orion, M 42, as photographed by the 100-inch telescope. A cloud of gas surrounds several very hot stars in the star cluster deep within the nebula. M 42 is visible to the naked eye as the middle star in the sword of Orion the Hunter.
Hale Observatories

erally agreed that physical processes involving enormous amounts of energy are taking place in the centers of galaxies.

In 1977, astronomers found evidence that such activity is happening in our own galactic center. Despite the great dust clouds hiding the center of the Milky Way, radio and infrared waves being emitted from there can get through these clouds. Scientists on Earth can pick up these waves with special equipment, study them, and learn more about what is going on in the nucleus of our galaxy. By analyzing these studies, astronomers say that there appears to be a mysterious ring-shaped structure of matter that goes all around the center of the Milky Way. It seems to be rotating. It is also moving away from the galactic center at the rate of about 100 miles per second. This ring is presently about 1200 light-years in diameter, but it is expanding outward—a portion of it toward the Earth. What caused the ring? One scientist thinks it may have been a gigantic explosion that happened about 400,000 years ago. He believes that what exploded may have had two million times the mass of our sun. (*Mass* is the amount of matter a body contains; it is not the same as *size.*)

Could this mysterious expanding ring of matter be potentially dangerous to future generations on Earth? Scientists do not know, but they are keeping a close watch on its progress.

2
TYPES OF GALAXIES

At first the existence of huge systems of stars outside our Milky Way galaxy was only suspected. It *was* known that faint hazy patches of light called "spiral nebulae" lay beyond our own star system. Could they be made up of stars? One early scientist gave these nebulae the picturesque name of island universes, a term no longer used by astronomers. Many of these early astronomers had little doubt that some of these nebulae were really made up of stars. They also knew that only with more powerful telescopes could the individual stars in an island universe be made out.

Then, in 1925, the American astronomer Edwin P. Hubble made photographs of nebulae that showed individual stars in them. Thus, the existence of extragalactic nebulae—galaxies outside the Milky Way—was proved beyond all doubt. During the next ten years, Hubble pushed the exploration of extragalactic space even farther. He found some of the nearer galaxies to be on the order of millions of light-years away. Later, using the 100-inch telescope on Mount Wilson to its limit, he located more distant galaxies a thousand times

farther away. Since then astronomers using the 200-inch telescope on Mount Palomar have photographed galaxies that appear to be billions of light-years distant from our Milky Way.

Long before Hubble's brilliant work, astronomers began to make catalogs of nebulae and clusters of stars. The first was published in 1771 by the French astronomer Charles

A mosaic of our Milky Way galaxy composed of several wide-angle photographs. *Hale Observatories*

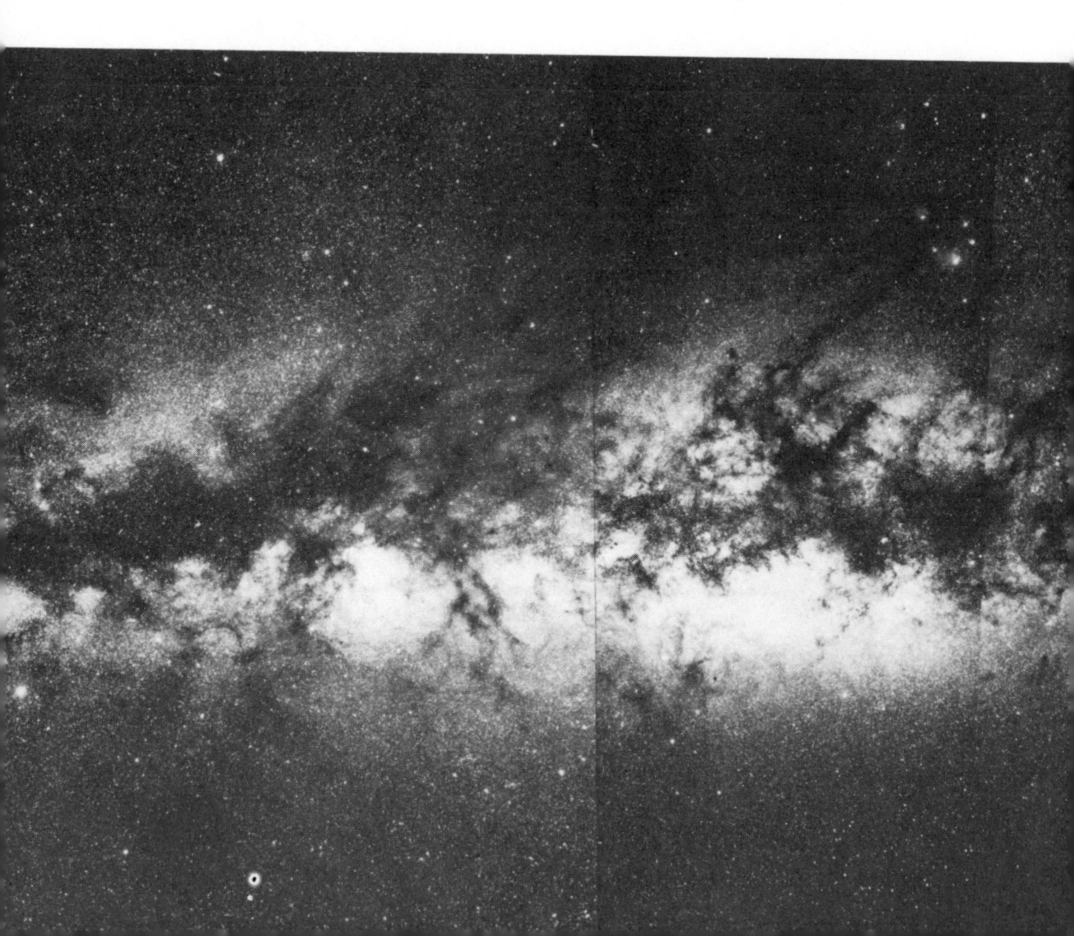

A model of the Milky Way galaxy, as seen edge on. Note position of the sun.

Messier. Messier's numbers for the brightest objects he listed are still in use today. For example, the great nebula in Andromeda, which we now know to be a galaxy, is called Messier 31, or M 31, because it is number 31 in Messier's catalog.

Another catalog system that astronomers use is the New General Catalog, or NGC. The *new* part of the catalog's title is hardly so today, for it was first published by the Irish astronomer John L. Dreyer in 1888. Nevertheless, the NGC numbers are very much in general use by modern astronomers. The brighter objects listed by Messier also have NGC numbers. For example, the Andromeda galaxy is NGC 224 as well as M 31. Besides the Messier and NGC numbers, astronomers sometimes use other cataloging systems.

Catalog numbers are useful in telling one galaxy from an-

The spiral galaxy M 33. Edwin Hubble studied nearby spirals to prove the existence of galaxies outside our own. M 33 belongs to our local group of galaxies. *Hale Observatories*

other in the heavens, especially when more than one is located in the same constellation. Although ancient peoples grouped the stars in constellations that they thought formed pictures in the night sky, these stars are at different distances from the Earth. One star in a constellation may be small and close to the Earth while another is large and thousands of light-years away. Or the larger "star" may in reality be a whole galaxy. For example, there are four galaxies in the constellation Ursa Major, the Great Bear. They were cataloged in Messier's list as M 81, M 82, M 97, and M 101. In the constellation Pegasus, there are three galaxies: NGC 7331, NGC 7479, and NGC 7841.

Early astronomers, peering through their small telescopes, saw extragalactic nebulae (and galaxies) as faint patches of light. They could also see that some had a spiral shape while others appeared to be circular or elliptical. In this way, the galaxies began to be divided into classes. Yet even into the twentieth century, when stronger telescopes were available, there were apt to be disagreements about which galaxies belonged to what classification. Where one astronomer might see a faint galaxy as circular, another might classify it as a spiral. Again Edwin Hubble was the one who helped resolve the situation.

In 1925, the same year in which he found proof that galaxies existed beyond our own, Hubble proposed a new classification system for them. It has been accepted, with a few

A portion of the Andromeda galaxy showing resolution into stars. By making such photos, which showed individual stars, Hubble demonstrated beyond doubt that other galaxies lay beyond our own.
Lick Observatory

changes, by astronomers all over the world. Briefly, Hubble divided galaxies into four main classes: the ellipticals, which he abbreviated E; the normal spirals, S; the barred spirals, SB; and the irregular galaxies, I. Each has different characteristics.

E. Elliptical galaxies have a smooth structure, shading from a bright nucleus, or center, outward to vaguely defined edges. They are shaped like an ellipsoid, or squashed sphere. Ellipticals are composed mostly of stars. Because of their richness in stars, they are among the brightest of the galaxies when observed through a telescope. A number of these galaxies appear to be round, or almost so, and astronomers sometimes call them "spheroidal galaxies." However, they are still classed as ellipticals because of their richness in stars.

The diameters of the ellipticals rarely exceed 7500 light-years, a mere fraction of the width of our Milky Way, a spiral galaxy. One elliptical near our own galaxy has a diameter of only 3000 light-years. The nearest elliptical to us is about two million light-years away. While most ellipticals are small, a few are the largest, most massive, and most luminous galaxies known. One is the giant galaxy M 87 in Virgo. (Shown on page 32.)

The spiral galaxy NGC 7331, one of three galaxies in the constellation Pegasus. *Kitt Peak National Observatory*

S. All spiral galaxies are highly flattened, lens-shaped star systems with great arms spiraling about them. Some have big hubs with arms that whirl about close in to the center. Others have smaller hubs with arms that spiral loosely out from the center. Between these extremes are spirals with hubs and arms of varying sizes and thicknesses. Some have only two or three arms while others have multiple arms.

Among the bigger galaxies, the spirals are the most numerous. They can be observed as far out in the universe as astronomers can see with the most powerful telescopes. The

The elliptical galaxy NGC 147 is a member of our local group of galaxies. *Hale Observatories*

The galaxy M 49 (NGC 4472) in the constellation Virgo is a nearly circular elliptical galaxy. *Kitt Peak National Observatory*

great spiral galaxy in Andromeda is the closest to the Milky Way. It is only two million light-years away. Our own galaxy is a normal spiral and closely resembles the great Andromeda galaxy in size and shape.

SB. There are also spiral galaxies that appear to have a bright bar passing through their centers. They usually have two coiled arms extending from the ends of the barlike portion. These galaxies are known as "barred spirals." Astronomers believe the bars are great accumulations of dust and gas. Both normal and barred-spiral galaxies rotate about their nuclei in the same manner. When they are observed through telescopes, a great number of spirals seem to be elliptical in shape, due to the angle from which they are observed from our own star system. If an observer could look

The spiral galaxy NGC 4622, type Sb, in the constellation Centaurus. Within its remarkably smooth and thin spiral arms there are millions of bright young stars. The galaxy is 200 million light-years away from Earth. *Kitt Peak National Observatory*

straight down on them, however, they would appear as great whirling spirals.

In Hubble's system of galaxies, there are three stages—*a*, *b*, and *c*—among the spirals. As can be seen in the accom-

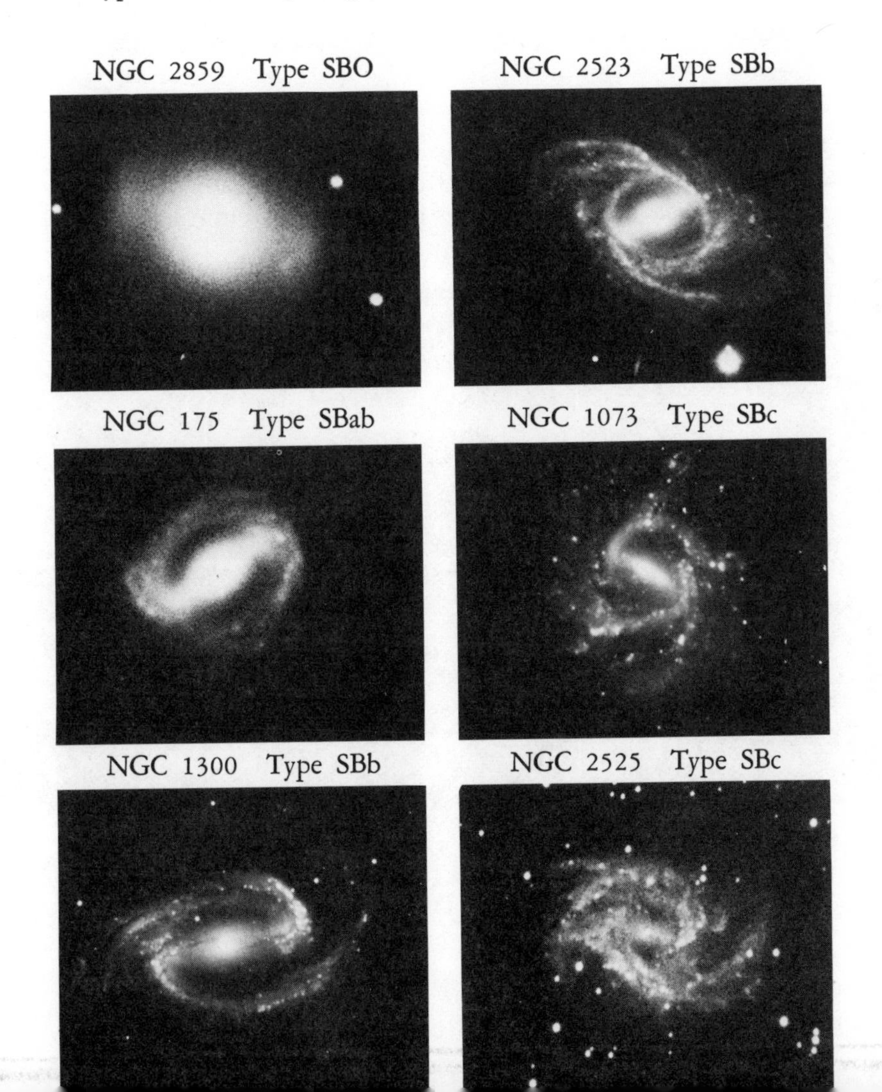

Six types of barred-spiral galaxies. *Hale Observatories*

panying diagram, the size of the hub is largest in *a* and smallest in *c*. As for the arms, they are thinnest and most closely coiled up in stage *a* and heavier and more opened up in stage *c*. Thus, if an astronomer classifies a galaxy as SBc, it would be a barred spiral with a small nucleus and thick, open arms.

I. Irregular galaxies are so called because they do not show any definite shape at all. Most of them have a flattened appearance and do not follow any regular pattern of rotation. Besides stars, the irregulars contain great clouds of gas and

In Hubble's system, there are three stages among normal and barred-spiral galaxies. The relative size of the nucleus decreases from *a* to *c* while the development of the arms increases from *a* to *c*.

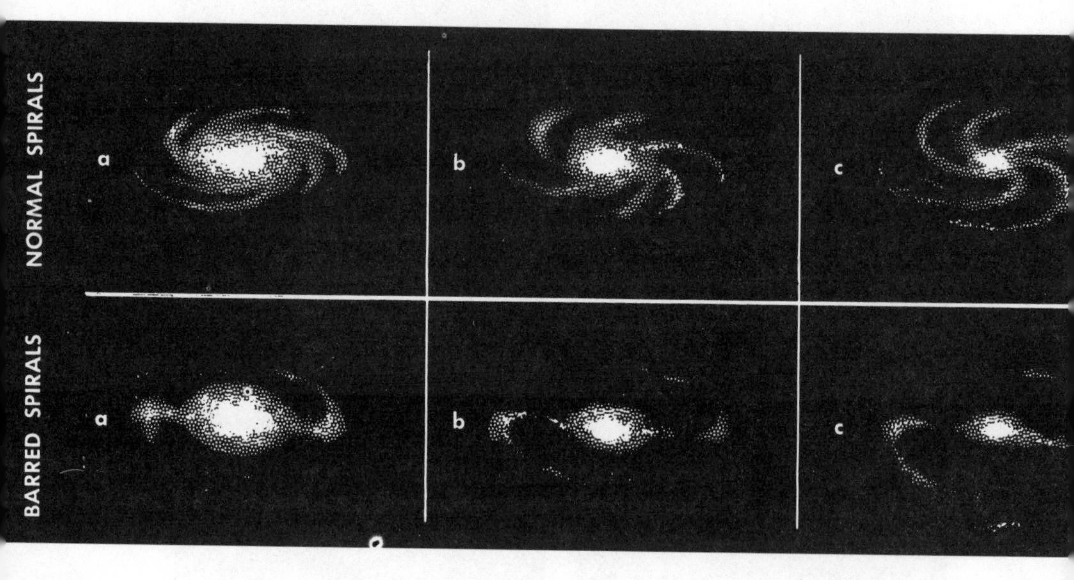

dust. They are also small in number, making up about 5 percent of all the visible external galaxies. The irregulars vary greatly in size. Some are no more than 8 or 9000 light-years across, while others exceed 30,000 light-years.

Two galaxies very near the Milky Way are irregulars.

The irregular galaxy NGC 3077 in the constellation Ursa Major. Note the odd pattern of dust lanes. *Kitt Peak National Observatory*

They are easily visible to the naked eye as faintly luminous patches; however, one must be in the southern hemisphere to observe them. They are the large Magellanic Cloud and the small Magellanic Cloud. Both are named after the famous explorer Ferdinand Magellan, one of the earliest men to sail the southern oceans and to observe these bodies. As irregulars go, these Magellanic Clouds are big. The large Cloud is over 30,000 light-years in diameter and is about 150,000 light-

The Large Magellanic Cloud is over 30,000 light-years in diameter and approximately 150,00 light-years distant from Earth.

Lick Observatory

years away. The small Cloud is farther away, about 170,000 light-years, and is some 25,000 light-years across.

Since Hubble first introduced his classification system, other types of galaxies have been discovered. One kind are the dwarf galaxies, so named for their small size. The smallest are only a few hundred light-years across; the largest are up to about 10,000 light-years in diameter. There are many of them, and astronomers think they may outnumber the

A dwarf galaxy showing resolution into stars. *Lick Observatory*

larger galaxies. Because of their comparatively tiny size, however, they are faint and hard to see through the most powerful telescopes. While some dwarfs appear to contain only stars, others seem to be made of dust and gas in which new stars are being born.

Astronomers today also speak of disk galaxies. Not to be confused with spirals or round-appearing ellipticals, a typical disk is large—about 100,000 light-years in diameter and 10 to 15,000 light-years thick. They are generally considered to be the flattest things in nature. As seen through telescopes, disks are well defined in outline compared to other types. Many astronomers now consider disk galaxies to be the final stage in the evolution of galaxies.

Some galaxies are classified not so much by shape as by the way they behave. If a galaxy has some outstanding characteristic that sets it apart from normal galaxies such as spirals and ellipticals, astronomers refer to it as a "peculiar galaxy." One kind of peculiar galaxy is a Markarian galaxy, named after its discoverer, B. D. Markarian, an Armenian astronomer. At present there are about 600 Markarians known. One of them, Markarian 132, is the brightest object in the universe. What sets the Markarians apart from other galaxies is

A peculiar galaxy in the constellation Ursa Major, NGC 3718.
Kitt Peak National Observatory

This peculiar galaxy in Perseus, NGC 1275, is called a "Seyfert galaxy" because it emits short bursts of intense radiation.
Kitt Peak National Observatory

that they send out abnormal amounts of ultraviolet radiation. Seyfert galaxies, named after their discoverer C. K. Seyfert, are another kind of peculiar galaxy. Seyferts are characterized by relatively short bursts of intense radiation.

Other galaxies are classified as peculiar because they interact with each other in some way. Astronomers call them "interacting galaxies"—two or more relatively near each other whose structural features are visibly distorted by some force between them. Such galaxies may be in the process of

Called the "whirlpool," this beautiful spiral galaxy, NGC 5194, is shown interacting with its small irregular companion, NGC 5195. Note luminous filaments extending from one to the other.

Hale Observatories

colliding with each other, or they may be the remains of a collision that took place in the past.

There is also evidence that one galaxy can pass right through another. In the mid-1970s, the American astronomer H. C. Arp published a startling photograph of a ring galaxy. Arp's theory is that the ring is the remnant of an ancient collision. The ring was formed by a massive body—perhaps itself a galaxy—passing through the disk of a larger galaxy.

About the same time, another ring galaxy was photographed by astronomers in the southern hemisphere. The picture shows two galaxies, which are about 300 million light-years away from Earth. The larger exhibits a gigantic ring about 180,000 light-years across. One astronomer believes the ring is made of younger stars recently formed from hydrogen gas surrounding the central galaxy. He thinks this star formation may have been triggered when the smaller galaxy passed through the disk of the larger galaxy. As is true of many interacting galaxies, these two are connected by a tail. Others are connected by luminous filaments, or bridges, that astronomers think are made of dust, gas, and possibly stars as well.

Galaxies in collision. These two galaxies, NGC 4038 and 9, in the constellation Corvus (the Crow) are seen here in the process of colliding with each other. Note how they mutually distort each other.
Mount Wilson and Palomar Observatories

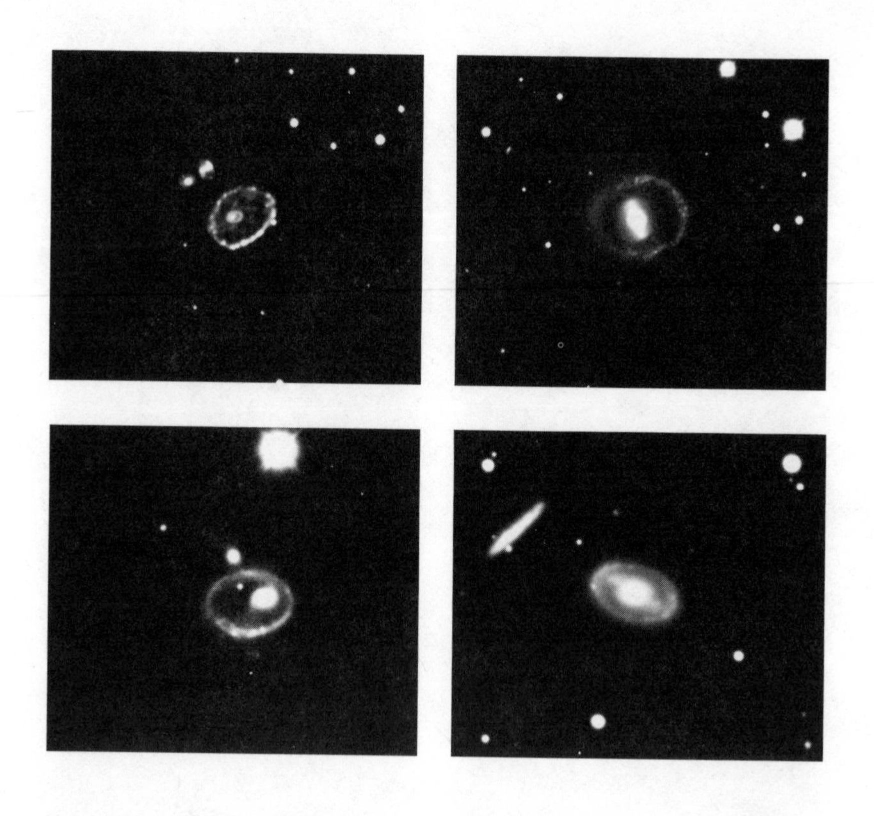

Four ring galaxies. These rare galaxies may be the result of collisions between pairs of galaxies. *Kitt Peak National Observatory*

Astronomers have known for several decades that many objects in the universe give off radio waves. Among them are galaxies. Radio galaxies fall into two classes: normal and peculiar. Normal radio galaxies are simply ordinary galaxies like our Milky Way, which give off some of their radiation as radio wave-lengths. Peculiar radio galaxies are ones that emit unusually large amounts of radio energy. Some of them resemble ordinary galaxies in all of their visual aspects. An example is the ordinary-appearing spiral NGC 1068, which gives off about 100 times more radio energy than other typical spirals.

A radio galaxy. This peculiar spiral galaxy, NGC 2623, is a source of radio noise. *Hale Observatories*

3
GROUPS, CLUSTERS, AND SUPERCLUSTERS

Except for interacting galaxies, the majority of galaxies in our universe are separated from one another by many thousands of light-years. However, they are not distributed evenly throughout space. Rather, all or nearly all occur in groups or clusters. A group of galaxies normally contains ten or more good-sized galaxies as well as a number of dwarfs. A cluster, on the other hand, may contain thousands of large galaxies and even more dwarfs.

Clusters of galaxies can be roughly divided into two classifications: regular and irregular. Regular clusters are spherical in shape and show a greater concentration of galaxies in

A small group of galaxies in Pegasus known as Stephen's Quintet. The pair in the center appear to be interacting with each other.
Lick Observatory

their center. They are rich in galaxies and usually have over a thousand very bright ones. Because they are actually globe shaped, some astronomers prefer to call them "globular clusters." A typical example is the famous cluster in Corona Borealis. Regular clusters consist almost entirely of elliptical and spiral galaxies.

Irregular clusters of galaxies are sometimes called "open clusters." Unlike the regulars, they have no special shape and do not have a concentration of galaxies in their center. Irregular clusters are more numerous than regular clusters, and they contain all kinds of galaxies—spirals, ellipticals, and

The globular cluster of galaxies in Corona Borealis. Most of the galaxies visible in this spectacular cluster are ellipticals. Ellipticals are more easily photographed than spirals of the same luminosity because of the ellipticals' greater compactness. *Hale Observatories*

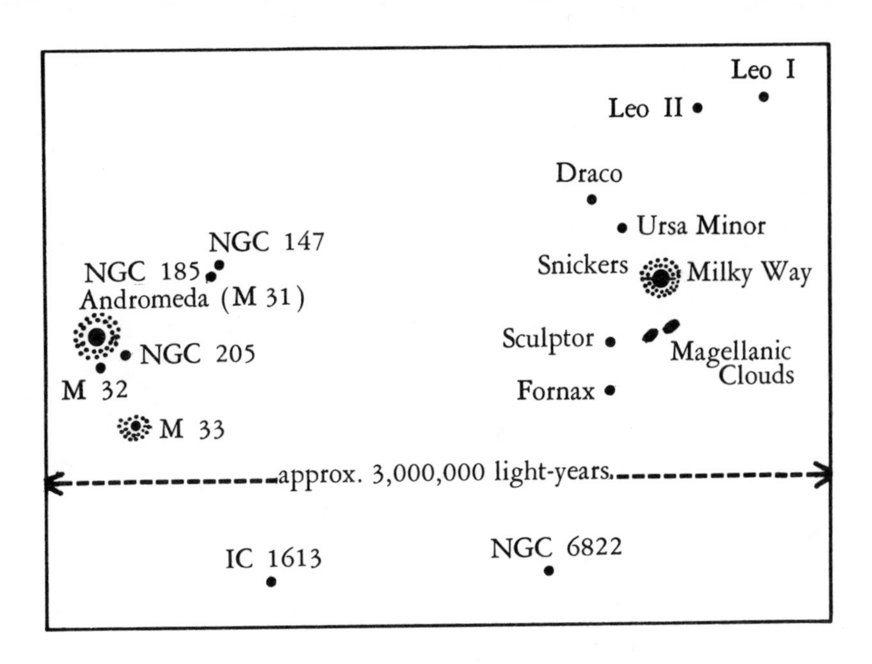

The local group of galaxies to which our own Milky Way galaxy belongs.

irregulars. They also range from rich collections of more than a thousand galaxies to small groups of a few dozen members or less.

An example of the latter is the local group, the small cluster of galaxies to which our Milky Way belongs. Our local group is oval shaped and contains five really large galaxies. The two largest are both spiral galaxies, our own and the Andromeda M 31 spiral. Our galaxy lies at one end of the egg-shaped group and is the second largest after M 31, which lies at the other end. In diameter, the local group is about three million light-years across.

In addition to M 31 and the Milky Way, the local group contains a third spiral, four irregulars, and ten ellipticals, of which six are dwarfs. Two of the irregulars are the large and small Magellanic Clouds. Astronomers think there may well be a few undiscovered members, especially in regions hidden by the vast dust clouds of the Milky Way.

The galaxies in the local group are approaching us or receding from us at different rates of speed, which astronomers have been able to measure. The Andromeda galaxy, for instance, is approaching us at about 160 miles per second, while the large Magellanic Cloud is retreating from us at about the same speed. The accompanying table gives the names, types, and diameters of galaxies in our local group.

Until 1975, astronomers thought that the galaxies nearest us were the two Magellanic Clouds. They also thought that the local group consisted of only seventeen members. But in that year they were amazed to discover an eighteenth. It is a small dwarf galaxy so close to the Milky Way that it is almost touching it! In fact, it is interacting with it right now. The gravitational effects of The Galaxy seem to be tearing stars away from the outer parts of the little dwarf galaxy. Its discoverer, M. Simonson, is an astronomer with a sense of humor. He has nicknamed the new galaxy Snickers, after the candy bar, because it is "peanuts" compared with the gigantic Milky Way galaxy.

Beyond the local group, at distances of a few times its

THE LOCAL GROUP

GALAXY	TYPE	DIAMETER IN LIGHT-YEARS
Milky Way	Sb	100,000
Large Mag. Cloud	Irr	30,000
Small Mag. Cloud	Irr	25,000
Ursa Minor	E (dwarf)	3,000
Sculptor	E (dwarf)	7,000
Draco	E (dwarf)	4,500
Fornax	E (dwarf)	22,000
Leo II	E (dwarf)	5,000
Leo I	E (dwarf)	5,000
NGC 6822	Irr	9,000
NGC 147	E	10,000
NGC 185	E	8,000
NGC 205	E	16,000
NGC 221 (M32)	E	8,000
IC 1613	Irr	16,000
Andromeda M31; (NGc 24)	Sb	130,000
NGC 598 (M33)	Sc	60,000

own diameter, there are similar small groups of galaxies. The nearest rich cluster of galaxies is the Virgo cluster. It is so named because it can be found in the direction of the constellation Virgo. Its distance is about sixty million light-years from us. The Virgo cluster appears as a great cloud, and photographs of it show nearly 3000 galaxies, although there are probably many more. The brightest of them are giant elliptical galaxies and large spirals. The faintest are dwarf

The cluster of galaxies in Virgo. Thousands of galaxies form a rich, loose, irregular cluster that appears to have no central concentration. This kind of cluster contains all types of galaxies.

Kitt Peak National Observatory

ellipticals more or less like the Sculptor and Fornax galaxies in our local group.

The Virgo cloud is an example of a rich irregular cluster of galaxies. Its structure is very complex. There are several dense subcondensations of galaxies within it as well as many double and triple galaxies (galaxies that are probably interacting with each other). Some astronomers think that possibly it might not even be a single cluster, but two at comparatively slight distances from one another. Other large clusters are those that lie beyond the constellations Corona Borealis and Coma Berenices (Bernice's Hair). Over 8500 galaxies have been counted in the latter cluster.

Astronomers have counted several thousand galaxies within about seventy million light-years of the Milky Way. Many of them are grouped into the Virgo cluster and a few

The large cluster of galaxies in Coma Berenices. It contains over 1000 members. Regular clusters of this kind generally include a large number of S and E galaxies and are often sources of X-ray radiation.
Kitt Peak National Observatory

other smaller irregular clusters. Most of the rest belong to small clusters, or groups, like our local group. Beyond the seventy million light-year mark, galaxies begin to thin out and are scarce in space until much larger distances are reached. For this reason, many astronomers believe that this immense collection of clusters and groups itself comprises a cluster of clusters. One prominent astronomer has named it the local supercluster. Its overall diameter is believed to be between 100 and 150 million light-years. It is also suspected that the local supercluster is flattened and is rotating.

What lies beyond the supercluster of which we are a part? Astronomers think there must be further small groups of galaxies, but they are not conspicuous to us. However, distant clusters have been observed to lie billions of light-years from our Milky Way, and there is evidence that they may be parts of supersystems like our own local supercluster.

4
THE AGE AND EVOLUTION OF GALAXIES

How old are the galaxies? Are some older than others, or are they all in the same stage of evolution? Are some galaxies dying while others are being born? Does a galaxy's environment have anything to do with its development? Do different galaxies have different histories? These are just a few of the questions that modern astronomers are trying to answer.

It is the common belief of astronomers today that galaxies do develop and evolve. Why do they think so? For one thing, they say, we live in a universe that is constantly changing. Nothing seems to be static or immobile. Why then shouldn't these most mammoth things in nature also undergo growth and change?

Another reason for this belief concerns the origin of the universe. The theory most widely held today—the big-bang theory—states that the universe began with a tremendous explosion about fifteen billion years ago and that the galaxies formed about ten billion years ago. Before that there were no galaxies, only evenly spread-out primordial material such as gas. This concept led many thinkers to believe that galaxies all began at the same time—and that they have all undergone a more or less parallel development ever since. However, the galaxies that astronomers saw through more powerful telescopes presented an array of different shapes. This observation changed their thinking, for the different shapes suggested that galaxies seem to be in different stages of evolution. Some appear older than others.

It is impossible, of course, to watch a galaxy evolve the way we can watch a flower sprout, grow, mature, and die. Galaxies take many millions of years to undergo change. Nevertheless, astronomers have evidence—based on radiation received from galaxies—that at least some galaxies may be younger than ten billion years, and younger by different amounts. So the question among astronomers today is not whether galaxies evolve, but how. One scientist has called this question "one of the more challenging problems in modern astronomy."

The stars of which galaxies consist are formed from what astronomers call the "interstellar medium"—the gas and dust between stars. The major vehicle for the study of galactic evolution and how environment may or may not affect it is gas, the gas within a given galaxy and in the space surrounding it. As more and more stars form, the gas is used up because it condenses to make the stars and is slowly changed into new elements. If other things are equal, then the galaxies that still have a lot of gas are younger than those with many stars that don't. When a galaxy uses up its gas, or when its gas is driven out of it by intergalactic material encountered in space, the formation of stars ceases. At this point, the now-gasless galaxy reaches the final stages of its life.

Up until a few years ago, most astronomers believed that the evolution of a galaxy went like this: A galaxy begins as a huge mass of gas and dust in space. The mass condenses until a dense hub, or nucleus, forms and starts to rotate. In time, arms from the whirling mass form and a spiral or barred spiral develops. After millions of years the arms close in toward the center of the galaxy. All the while, the dust and gas—almost all of it hydrogen—is being used up as new stars form. Eventually the arms of the spiral tighten in closer and closer to the hub until the galaxy ends its life as an elliptical. So logical and correct did this evolutionary process seem that it appeared in most textbooks and encyclopedias, complete with diagrams.

Today, however, astronomers think the process happens the other way around. As the great cloud of gas, dust, and newly forming stars condenses, it does so not as a spiral but as an elliptical galaxy. After rotation starts, the elliptical develops in time the arm pattern as a spiral galaxy. Over millions of years, the galaxy loses its arm pattern as gas is stripped from it or is used up in star formation. Finally, the galaxy evolves to its last stage, not an elliptical as previously thought but a featureless disk galaxy.

Yet much can happen between the birth and death of galaxies that still baffles astronomers. Obviously the galaxies are in different stages of evolution. Some are dim; some are bright. Their shapes differ. A recent study of 180 galaxies has shown that the environment in which a galaxy is born has a lot to do with how it evolves. Yet gas within and around galaxies remains the clue that astronomers use to deduce how they began and developed. The presence or absence of such gas and its chemical composition give astronomers much information about the mysteries of galactic evolution.

If the galaxies are so far away, how can astronomers possibly know anything about the chemical composition of the gas within and around them? Astronomers use an instrument called a "spectroscope" to study and analyze the light that comes from the galaxies. When the light from a galaxy passes through the spectroscope, it splits up into a colored band called a "spectrum." By studying the light spectrums of galaxies, scientists can tell which chemicals are present in the gas and matter of galaxies. In addition, astronomers can tell much about certain galaxies by studying the radio waves that emanate from them.

The chemistry of the gas in and around the stars in galaxies also gives astronomers clues about galactic evolution. In the early history of the universe, all gas was hydrogen and helium. Supposedly, the first galaxies began as clouds of these gases collapsed under their gravity into elliptical-shaped masses. Hydrogen and helium were the raw material from which the first stars were formed. This first generation of stars began to burn and glow by a complex process called "nuclear fusion." In this process, the light hydrogen gas was eventually changed into heavier chemical elements such as metals. Many of these first-generation stars exploded; others were swept by stellar winds, radiation from other stars. In this way, new material was thrown back into the galaxy, and the galactic gas gradually became enriched with heavier elements. Scientists think this same process may still be going on and that new galaxies are being born now just as they were early in the history of the universe.

By studying the concentration of heavy elements in a

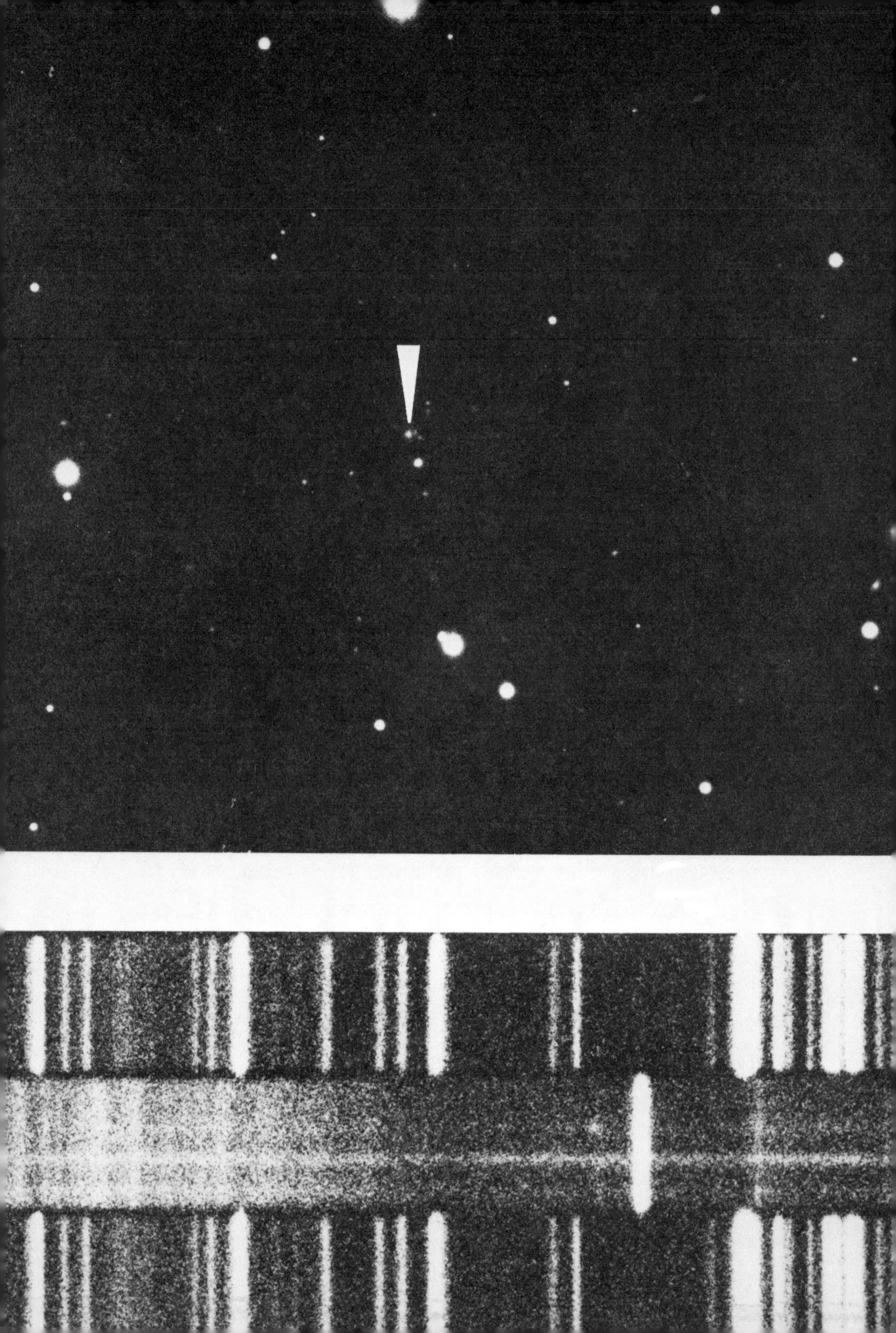

galaxy's gas, especially metals, astronomers can find clues to its evolutionary stage. Stars of second and later generations are already enriched in heavy metals when they are born, and this characteristic can distinguish them from first-generation stars. Also, where the brightest stars are found in a galaxy, there should be the heaviest concentration of metals. In a recent survey of several dozen galaxies, some astronomers made this finding.

Astronomers further think that some galaxies can be swept clean of their gas by shock waves that form as they rush through the intergalactic medium. This occurrence would have an important environmental effect on their evolution. In the mid-1970s, a group of astronomers studied twenty-five galaxies that, by their appearance, had been recently stripped of their gas. They were smooth-armed spirals, some of which showed weak arm patterns. If the new evolutionary theory were correct, the ones with the weak arm patterns should be more evolved (closer to featureless disks) than the ones with stronger arms. The spectrographic evidence turned out to fit the theory. The processes of star evolution and metal

A photograph and spectrum of galaxy 3C 295 in the constellation Bootes. Until 1975, 3C 295 was thought to be the most distant galaxy known—5 billion light-years away from Earth. The 3C designation refers to the Third Cambridge catalog of radio sources.

Hale Observatories

enrichment should make a galaxy's spectrum redder as it evolves, and the spectrums of the galaxies with the weak arm patterns were redder than those of the stronger-armed ones.

Yet astronomers know that there are some cases that cannot be so easily explained on the basis of environmental influences. For example, some spirals have less surface brightness than is normal for spiral galaxies. Low surface brightness implies fewer stars. Would the lack of many stars in these galaxies suggest that they have been forming stars for the same ten billion years as all the others, only at a slower rate? Or would it mean that the starmaking began at a much later date?

Astronomers recently studied this situation. They found that the galaxies with low surface brightness have several times the hydrogen gas than that of the brighter spirals, which would be the case with the formation of fewer stars. Their spectrums were also bluer. Thus, these spirals had predominantly first-generation stars and their starmaking began later.

Astronomers have also wondered about disk galaxies on the edge of clusters versus those located in the middle. Another recent study of two clusters showed that the disks in the outer portions of the clusters were generally larger than those in the center. A larger disk, of course, would mean more stars. Did the starmaking go on longer in the larger disks? Scientists think perhaps the bigger disks are surrounded by gas clouds that for some reason are not disturbed by the intergalactic medium through which the galaxies travel. At any rate, astronomers strongly suspect that starmaking is triggered in different galaxies at different times. However, they still have much to learn about the triggering mechanism.

In the survey of 180 galaxies that was done in the mid-1970s, scientists found out an important fact about galactic evolution. It was discovered that galaxies in clusters that have a high density of intergalactic matter tend to age prematurely. Starmaking for them ceases sooner than for galaxies with less intergalactic matter. As these galaxies rush through this denser material, it is thought that strong pressure waves are set up. They may drive out of the galaxy the hydrogen from which new stars could form and bring starmaking to an early end.

5
GALACTIC CENTERS, QUASARS, AND BLACK HOLES

Superviolence! That is what astronomers think the scene must be like at the center of galaxies. They are generally agreed that the physical processes going on there involve amounts of energy so enormous as to stagger the imagination.

There is plenty of evidence to support this belief. The nuclei of galaxies look brighter than their outer regions in all ranges of electromagnetic radiation. Observation of radio waves of galactic centers reveals that there are large regions of radio-emitting matter that go far beyond the confines of the visible galaxy. All of this evidence points to fantastic quantities of material continually being pumped out of galactic centers by whatever violent processes are taking place there.

In galaxies that have heavier and better developed nuclei, there is even more activity. Proof has been found of such activity in a number of nearby bright galaxies. Astronomers have observed gas being expelled by their nuclei and moving away into space at very high speeds. Also, some inner portions of galaxies have been observed to be moving away from their nuclei. Many astronomers now tend to think that a spiral-structured galaxy indicates increased activity at its center. The gas expelled from the nucleus is believed to gather more gas as it passes outward into the arms.

Galactic nuclei that explode and divide, throwing out great quantities of material, are also found in many Markarian galaxies. Some of this activity is known to occur on a very quick time scale. One such galaxy, Markarian 6, is a recent instance. During 1969 there was no evidence that anything unusual was going on in this galaxy. Suddenly, in 1970, an explosion began and spectroscopes revealed that great amounts of hydrogen gas were being pumped out of Markarian 6 at speeds of nearly 2000 miles per second! Possibly it was being ejected toward the Earth.

Yet gas is not the only thing that galactic nuclei may be throwing out. A superassociation of stars is a group of stars so large that it approaches the size of a dwarf galaxy. At present, one such superassociation appears to be moving rapidly away from the center of a Markarian galaxy. Some astronomers believe it may have been ejected from the nucleus. One prominent astronomer thinks it possible that whole galaxies may be ejected from large galactic nuclei.

For nearly two decades, astronomers have observed some strange objects that look like stars and which may have their origin in galactic centers. These objects are called "quasi-stellar sources," or simply "quasars" for short. (*Quasi* means *something like.*) Unlike stars, however, these objects send out very strong radio waves. Their light also seems to be different from normal starlight.

Quasars are among the most distant of known objects. Being so far away and yet visible, they are thus the brightest bodies in the universe. In photographs they appear dim only because they are so greatly removed from Earth. Astronomers have calculated that a typical quasar is about ten light-years across—much larger than even the largest stars. To date, scientists have been unable to explain how quasars can emit so much light and radio energy—energy at rates characteristic of about 100 galaxies.

One of the most important astronomical questions today is whether quasars have any relationships to galaxies. A number of scientists think they do. Yet most quasars are extremely distant; some scientists believe them to be at the very edge of the visible universe. Looking out into space is always looking backward in time, for the light of such objects as quasars takes billions of years to reach us. Quasars would appear, therefore, to be largely relics of the early days of the universe. If so, scientists must ask what quasars have to tell us about its early history and evolution.

Some astronomers suggest that quasars are qualitatively different from other celestial phenomena, with a physics and meaning all their own. Other astronomers, however, believe that quasars are not different phenomena at all but happenings common to the centers of galaxies. They say that we see the most spectacular of them as quasars. Since the less energetic don't shine as obviously, we do not associate them with galactic centers. Moreover, say these scientists, quasars may be an early stage in the evolution of galaxies, a stage before the extended parts such as arms form. Or they may be galactic nuclei that never developed into whole galaxies, a kind of galactic evolutionary freak.

Have astronomers found any quasars that seem to be surrounded by a galaxy? Not as yet. However, many of them believe that by studying the so-called BL Lacertae objects a possible link may be found between quasars and galactic nuclei. These bright objects have similarities to quasars but appear to be more spread out in space and are highly variable in the energy they emit.

A number of astronomers have speculated further about

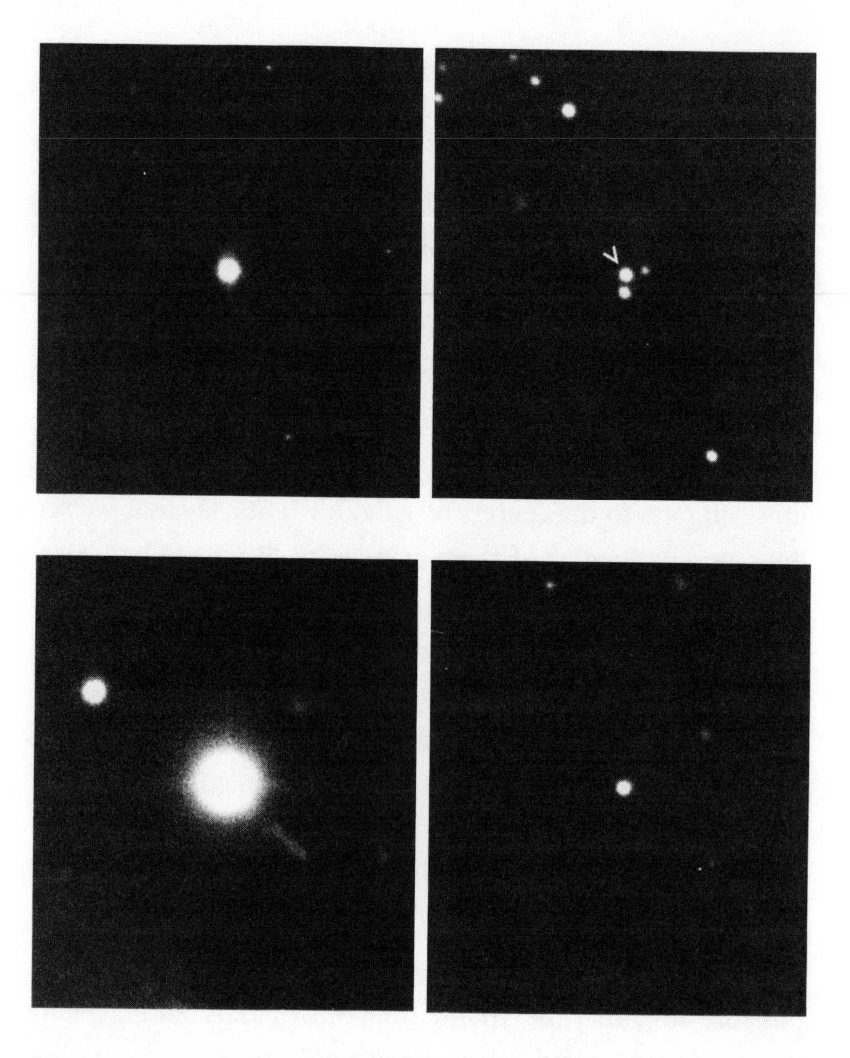

Four quasars (quasi-stellar sources). Among the most distant of all objects, quasars are much larger than stars and emit fantastic quantities of light and radio energy. A typical quasar sends out as much energy as 100 galaxies! *Hale Observatories*

the nature of galactic centers. They have suggested that the superviolent activity in the nuclei of galaxies is caused by a gigantic black hole at the center. What exactly is this oddly named phenomenon?

When a massive star nears the end of its life and runs out of nuclear fuel, the immense forces of gravity that have been held in check within the star suddenly become dominant. In other words, the star collapses in on itself. Matter produced by this mammoth gravitational crunch is unbelievably dense; one cubic inch of this compacted material could weigh up to hundreds of billions of tons! Even a tiny speck of such matter could not be supported by the Earth. If it could somehow be transported to Earth, it would sink effortlessly through the crust, mantle, and core of the planet like a heavy cleaver through warm butter. The death of such a star, which may have been some sixteen million miles in diameter, means that it has collapsed to a diameter of only a few miles.

In a stellar object of this type, the gravitational field on its surface grows so great that no light or other radiation can escape from it. In effect, it disappears from the visible universe. That is why astronomers refer to this phenomenon as a black hole. If a flashlight were shone directly on a black hole, nothing would be seen because the light would be sucked right down its superpowerful gravitational drain, never to be reflected back to the eye. One scientist described a black hole this way: "The star digs a hole, jumps in, and pulls the hole in after it."

Some astronomers are now proposing that the basis of the quasar phenomenon is an immense black hole inhabiting the heart of a galaxy. These black holes would form out of supermassive stars clustered in the galactic center. Once such a black hole is formed, its gravitational field would completely dominate the portion of the galactic core near it. It would also increase the density of stars around it. This supermassive phenomenon would force stars to orbit around it and would tear small stars apart. It would swallow whole stars the size of our sun. Larger stars would burst under violent tidal forces and be swallowed piece by piece. There would be constant star collisions. Some scientists believe the appetite of such a black hole would be voracious; it would have to be fed constantly. The dense group of stars surrounding the black hole would nourish the phenomenon continuously, replacing what falls down it. More and more stars would constantly come under its irresistible gravitational field.

Is there at present any factual evidence that black holes actually do occupy the centers of galaxies? There is. In the late 1970s, astronomers from the California Institute of Technology used three powerful radio telescopes to observe the galaxy NGC 6251. They concluded that the phenomenon found in the nucleus of that galaxy could best be explained by the presence of a supermassive black hole. They estimate its mass could be approximately 100 million times that of our sun!

At about the same time, other astronomers came forward with additional information regarding another galaxy. It was a familiar one long observed and studied by astronomers. In the eighteenth century, Charles Messier listed it as number 87 in his catalog. A member of the nearest cluster of galaxies to our own, the Virgo cluster, M 87 is also known to astronomers as NGC 4486. It has been of interest to astronomers because it is a peculiar galaxy, but it emits far more energy than galaxies of its class normally do. When astronomers studied M 87, they concluded that there is indeed some mammoth object in the galaxy's nucleus that could be a black hole.

In part, the presence of such an object was determined by studying the velocities of stars in M 87, particularly in the immediate neighborhood of the galactic center. The object was to look for large numbers of faster moving stars near the center rather than toward the edges. They would indicate the presence of a vast amount of matter in the nucleus. Why? Because such matter would have to be present to hold the stars in toward the nucleus. If the object were a black hole, the inward-falling stellar material could be generating immense

The giant elliptical galaxy M 87 in Virgo may be the site of a black hole.
Hale Observatories

amounts of radiation. It would act as a huge pump for expelling the great quantities of matter that seem to be coming out of M 87.

In scanning the speeds of stars in M 87, the astronomers

found that those near the center were moving much faster than those in the outer areas. While these astronomers aren't claiming that the results prove that there is a black hole at the galaxy's center, they do suggest it is a strong possibility. If the supermassive object is a black hole, its mass could be about five billion times that of our sun!

6
THE EXPANDING UNIVERSE

If the galaxies beyond our Milky Way are so distant, how can astronomers calculate how far away they are? One method is by observing the brightness of certain kinds of stars within the galaxy. To do so, an astronomer picks out variable stars in the galaxy. These stars are ones that change their brightness in a known amount of time. The astronomer already knows from the rate at which they change how bright these stars can get. Then he observes how bright the stars look in the galaxy at the moment. Using a formula based on

A faint cluster of galaxies well over a billion light-years from Earth. If the Andromeda Galaxy were moved out to this distance, it would look no larger or brighter than the brightest members of this cluster.
Hale Observatories

the two degrees of brightness, the time elapsed between them, and the speed of light, the astronomer can figure out by mathematics how far away the galaxy is.

Astronomers, however, are the first to admit that the brightness method is subject to error. For example, in the space between galaxies great dust clouds can absorb the light energy passing through it. In that case, the brightness of the galaxy's variable stars is dimmed, and calculations would indicate the galaxy in question is farther away than it really is.

In the mid-1970s, a new invention appeared that has been a boon to astronomical studies of faint objects like distant galaxies. It is called an "image-intensifier tube." Even the most powerful telescopes cannot make much of a distant faint object in the heavens. It may be even fainter than the night-sky background illumination. When such observations are wanted, the image-intensifier tube can be used to convert light to electronic impulses, which are stored by a computer. The computer then builds up an image by heightening contrast during successive scans across the faint object until a readable picture develops. The device is especially helpful in getting more accurate spectrograms from spectroscopes.

Using the image intensifier in 1975, an astronomer in California determined that a galaxy called 3C 123 is eight billion light-years away. The most distant galaxy previously known is five billion light-years away and was discovered in 1960.

Although 3C 123 is not the most distant object known—a few quasars are farther away—it is the most distant galaxy and so will give important clues to the history and development of other galaxies in the universe. When the light that now reaches us left 3C 123, the Earth did not yet exist. Nor did the sun. Astronomers are generally agreed that our sun is a later-generation star. There should be few or none like it in 3C 123. When the light from it is examined, astronomers believe it will indicate that the galaxy's stars are in early stages of development.

So far away are the galaxies outside our own that they cannot be observed to move in the heavens. Even those closest to us in the local group cannot be seen to change their position. If you were an astronomer and you kept watching the Great Galaxy in Andromeda (M 31) every night for ten years, you would not see it move.

Yet astronomers know that galaxies are in motion. Some are traveling toward us; others are moving away. How can astronomers tell which are approaching and which receding? They can do so with the spectroscope.

As we know, when the light from a galaxy enters the spectroscope, it breaks up into a colored band, or spectrum. At one end of the spectrum is red, at the other, blue. The spectrum is crisscrossed by patterns of dark vertical lines. Astronomers check the galaxy's line patterns against those usually produced by the same kinds of gases on Earth. They watch carefully to see whether the lines in the galaxy's pattern have shifted as compared with those in its normal spectrum.

If astronomers see that there is a shift in the dark-line patterns, they know that the galaxy is traveling either toward us or away from us. If the dark lines shift toward the blue end of the spectrum, the galaxy is traveling toward us. But if they shift toward the red end of the spectrum, the galaxy is traveling away from us. Scientists refer to this shift toward the red end of the spectrum as a red shift.

What about our sister galaxies in the local group? Are they approaching us or receding from us? A few in the local group do show blue shifts. Aside from them, however, all the rest of the galaxies in the observable universe show red shifts. Apparently the entire universe of galaxies is moving apart.

There is more to the story, however. Astronomers have also found out that the farther away galaxies are, the bigger their red shifts appear to get. What does this finding mean? Simply that the farther away a galaxy is, the more rapidly it is moving away from the Earth. Therefore, most astronomers today believe that the universe is constantly expanding.

One might be tempted to think, since all the galaxies outside the local group are traveling away from the Earth, that our own galaxy is at the center of this expanding universe. But this is not so. Imagine that you have a balloon with dozens of dots marked on it with a Magic Marker. If you blow up the balloon, its surface expands. The dots move farther and farther apart. Now pretend that the Milky Way galaxy is one of these dots. All the other dot "galaxies" get farther away from your own, no matter which one you have chosen. Thus, you can see that no single galaxy could be

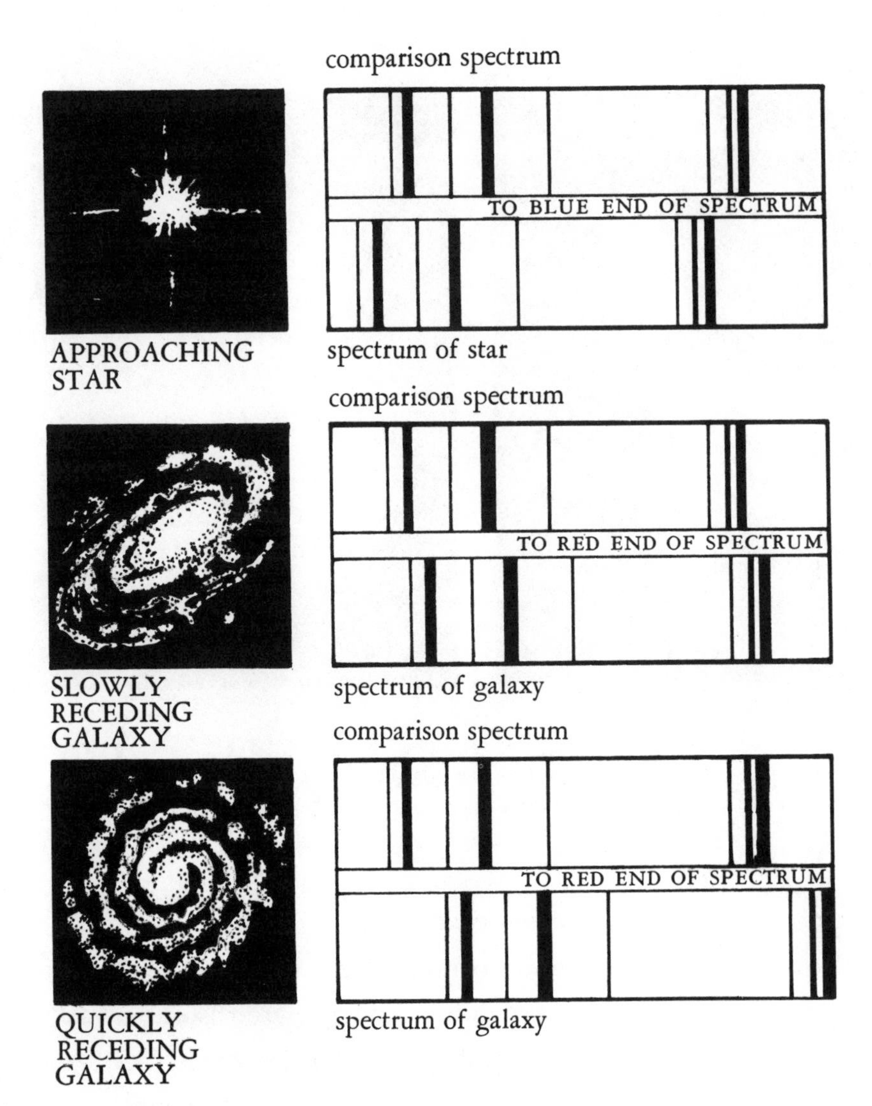

Astronomers can find out a galaxy's directional motion and speed by comparing its spectrum with a laboratory spectrum of substances that make up the galaxy.

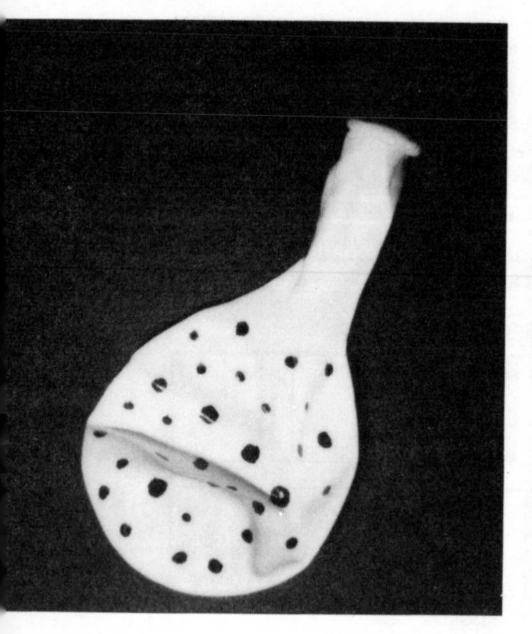

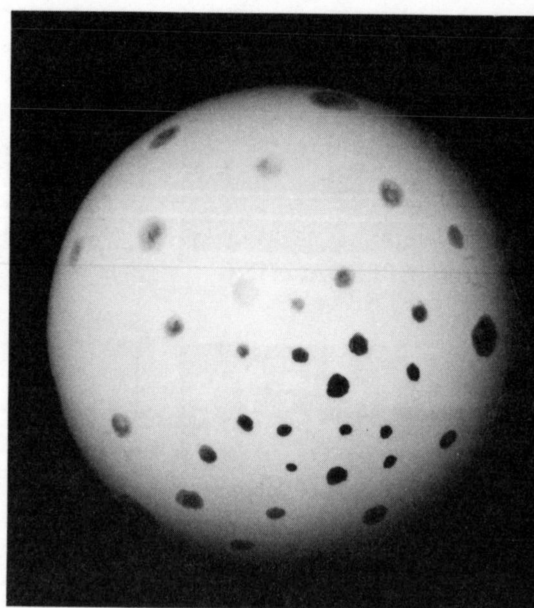

The galaxies of our universe are rushing away from each other in much the same manner as dots on an expanding balloon.

said to be at the universe's center. In fact, most astronomers believe that the universe has no center at all.

The galaxies of the expanding universe are rushing away from us at very high velocities. The nearer ones, such as those in the Virgo cluster, are traveling at about 700 miles a second. Those much farther away, say at distances of about five billion light-years, are traveling at speeds of about 90,000 miles per second, about half the speed of light.

Astronomers believe that some galaxies even farther away are hurtling through space at speeds approaching the speed of light itself. Thus the light they are now emitting can never reach the Earth. Nor could their radio waves ever reach us either, for they travel at the same speed that light does. Therefore, we on Earth can never observe all the galaxies that exist in the universe. We can only observe those that are traveling at speeds much less than the velocity of light. As a result, scientists often talk of the observable universe rather than just the universe. They believe that what we can observe is only a portion of the entire universe.

If the whole universe extends ever outward into space, how far does it go? Does it extend outward forever? Or does it perhaps reach an end at some incredibly remote region where no more galaxies exist? If there is such a place, what lies beyond *it*? Astronomers can only speculate about such questions, and the answers may ever elude them.

There is a more practical question, however, that astronomers are hoping to answer—perhaps in the near future. Since the classic work of Edwin Hubble and others in the early decades of this century, astronomers have accepted the notion that the universe is expanding. In most scientists' minds, this concept confirms the big-bang theory—that some fifteen billion years ago a gigantic, tightly packed superatom exploded, its material condensed into galaxies, and these galaxies have been moving outward into space ever since. The question is simply this: Will the universe, which consists of the galaxies, expand forever?

The key to the answer lies in the galaxies themselves. If the galaxies continue to rush away from each other, the universe will grow thinner and thinner. It will also get colder and colder. The stars will run out of nuclear fuel and collapse into lifeless bodies devoid of heat and light, burned-out stars. In the far future, even the voracious galactic centers—perhaps containing black holes—would run out of material to feed them and die. If expansion continues, it will result in the death of the universe.

However, there is one force operating in the universe that some astronomers think will prevent this end. It is the force of gravity, which attracts all of the bodies in the universe to each other. The chief bodies in the universe are, of course, the galaxies. It is the belief of many scientists that the mutual attraction of the galaxies for each other will gradually slow down the expansion of the universe. If this deceleration takes place soon enough, the expansion must stop and begin to contract, resulting eventually in a closed universe. If it doesn't and expansion continues, the result is an open universe.

Which will happen? For decades, astronomers have argued back and forth about the question, hoping to find some evidence for deceleration. They are still not in agreement. In the late 1970s, however, two sets of observations by astronomers have given the argument a couple of unexpected twists. The first was a series of observations of distant galaxies that seemed to indicate that the expansion might be proceeding in a lopsided manner rather than uniformly spherical as everyone had always assumed. The second and even more surprising set of observations seemed to show that the universe is accelerating its expansion!

In such studies, astronomers observe the red shifts of light from distant galaxies. In order to check whether the rate of expansion has changed over the eons or not, they look at the most distant and, therefore, most ancient galaxies. In doing so, they are looking back in time to see how things were moving in bygone eons. The results are then compared with evidence from nearby galaxies, which shows how things have been moving in more recent times.

After the studies in the late 1970s were completed and it appeared that almost no deceleration was going on in the universe, the astronomers realized they had overlooked something. To compare red shift data, they work with independent estimates of the distance of the galaxies. For this information, the brightness of the distant galaxies is compared to that of a similar class of nearer galaxies, which gives a measure of their distance from us. However, since looking at distant galaxies is looking far back into the past, the astronomers realized that they would have to correct for galactic evolution over a long period of time. When they

The cluster of galaxies in the constellation Hercules. The light we now see from these galaxies left them more than a half-billion years ago. Note the wide variety of galactic shapes in the cluster.
Kitt Peak National Observatory

calculated a realistic correction for this evolution and put it into their equations, the result confirmed that acceleration *was* going on.

These astronomers checked and rechecked their figures. Then they realized that they had not taken into account new evidence about the evolution of galaxies. The brightest galaxy in a cluster—one of those the astronomers were using in their survey—can swallow up nearby galaxies from time to time. Then, of course, the brightness of the swallowing galaxy is increased, counteracting the dimming effect of galactic evolution. When allowance was made for this phenomenon in their equations, the astronomers found that the acceleration factor disappeared. When other corrections were made in the figures for the shape of the expanding universe, it was found that the lopsided effect also vanished. So these astronomers have concluded that our expanding universe *is* decelerating slightly but probably too slowly ever to reverse its motion and collapse back on itself.

What lies in the future for our universe of galaxies? No one knows for certain. Neither do scientists know for sure whether the universe will ever come to an end. Yet much remains to be discovered about the processes at work in the fantastically energetic centers of galaxies. It may be that as astronomers learn more about the behavior of galaxies, they will unearth completely new ideas about the origin and future of the universe.

GLOSSARY

barred spiral galaxy • a spiral galaxy that appears to have a bright bar passing through its center.

big-bang theory • some fifteen billion years ago a gigantic, tightly packed superatom exploded, its material condensed into galaxies, and these galaxies have been moving outward into space ever since.

black hole • the complete gravitational collapse of a massive dying star resulting in compacted matter of fantastic density. The gravitational forces exerted by such a phenomenon are so strong that no matter or radiation can escape from it.

closed universe • theory that the expanding universe will decelerate, stop its expansion, and begin to contract.

cluster of galaxies • a system of galaxies containing several to thousands of member galaxies.

constellation • a configuration of stars named for a particular object, person, or animal, or the area of the sky assigned to a particular configuration. A constellation is *not* a galaxy.

core of a galaxy • the central portion, or nucleus, of a galaxy.

dwarf galaxies • small galaxies ranging from a few hundred light-years across up to 10,000 light-years in diameter.

disk galaxy • a large, very flat, featureless galaxy about 100,000 light-years in diameter, 10 to 15,000 light-years thick, and well defined in outline.

elliptical galaxy • a typically small galaxy shaped like an ellipsoid, or squashed sphere.

expanding universe • the apparent opening outward of the universe—much like a balloon that is being inflated—due to the galaxies flying away from each other at tremendous speeds.

galaxy • a large assemblage of stars; a typical galaxy contains millions to hundreds of billions of stars.

The Galaxy • our galaxy, the Milky Way.

globular cluster of galaxies • a globe-shaped cluster of galaxies.

group of galaxies • a small assemblage of galaxies, normally containing ten or more good-sized members.

hub • the central portion, or nucleus, of a galaxy.

interacting galaxies • two or more galaxies relatively near each other whose structural features are visibly distorted by some force between them.

image-intensifier tube • an electronic device used by astronomers to determine more accurately the distance from Earth of distant galaxies.

interstellar medium • the gas, dust, and other matter between stars.

irregular galaxy • a galaxy that shows no definite shape.

island universe • a historical synonym for a galaxy no longer used in astronomy.

light-year • the distance light travels in a vacuum in one year—about six trillion miles.

local group • the small assemblage of galaxies to which our Milky Way galaxy belongs.

Markarian galaxy • one of about 600 peculiar galaxies that emit abnormal amounts of ultraviolet radiation. Named after their discoverer, B. D. Markarian.

mass • a measure of the total amount of material in a body.

Messier catalog • a catalog of prominent galaxies prepared by Charles Messier in 1787.

Milky Way galaxy • the galaxy to which our sun and neighboring stars belong, consisting of billions of stars; also called our galaxy and The Galaxy.

nebula • a vast cloud of interstellar gas or dust.

New General Catalog (NGC) • a catalog of star clusters, nebulae, and galaxies compiled by J. L. Dreyer in 1888.

nuclear fusion • in a star, the complex process by which hydrogen atoms are converted into helium atoms, thus releasing tremendous quantities of energy.

nucleus of a galaxy • the central portion of a galaxy in which processes are going on involving tremendous amounts of energy; a galactic center.

open universe • a universe that continues to expand.

peculiar galaxy • a galaxy with some outstanding characteristic that sets it apart from normal galaxies such as spirals and ellipticals.

quasar • abbreviated name for *quasi-stellar object*; among the most distant of known objects, quasars are much larger than stars and emit abnormal amounts of visible radiation and radio energy.

radio galaxy • a galaxy that gives off some of its radiation as radio waves.

red shift • a shift of spectral lines toward the red end of the spectrum of the light from remote galaxies.

Seyfert galaxy • a kind of peculiar galaxy characterized by relatively short bursts of intense radiation. Named after its discoverer, C. K. Seyfert.

solar system • the system of the sun, its planets, and other objects revolving around the sun.

spectroscope • an instrument for directly viewing the spectrum of a light source such as a galaxy.

spectrum • the array of colors or wave lengths obtained when light from a source is dispersed, as in passing through the prism of a spectroscope.

spheroidal galaxy • an elliptical galaxy that appears almost round.

spiral galaxy • a highly flattened, lens-shaped galaxy with great arms spiraling about it.

superassociation of stars • a group of stars so large that it approaches the size of a dwarf galaxy.

supercluster of galaxies • an immense collection of clusters and groups of galaxies; the local supercluster to which our Milky Way belongs is believed to be between 100 and 150 million light-years across.

universe • all of creation; everything there is.

variable star • a star that changes its brightness or luminosity in a known amount of time.

INDEX

** indicates illustration*

ABOUT THE AUTHOR

Born in Glens Falls, New York, David C. Knight received his education both in this country and abroad. He earned his BA degree at Union College in Schenectady, New York, spent a year at the Sorbonne in Paris, then completed his studies at the Engineering Institute in Philadelphia and at the University of Pennsylvania.

Science has been one of Mr. Knight's major interests. He has worked as an editor and production man with Prentice-Hall and for sixteen years served as senior science editor at Franklin Watts. In addition to the many books he has written on scientific subjects, he has contributed a number of science articles to the *New Book of Knowledge.*

Mr. Knight currently lives in Dobbs Ferry, New York, with his wife and two daughters.